THE

PROCEEDINGS

OF TWO MEETINGS,

HELD IN BOSTON, ON THE 7TH & 14TH JULY,

TO PROTEST AGAINST THE

NOMINATION OF GEN. SCOTT,

FOR THE PRESIDENCY,

AND TO RECOMMEND

HON. DANIEL WEBSTER

FOR THAT OFFICE.

BOSTON:
PRINTED BY PRENTISS & SAWYER,
No. 11 Devonshire Street.
1852.

THE

PROCEEDINGS

OF TWO MEETINGS,

HELD IN BOSTON, ON THE 7TH & 14TH JULY,

TO PROTEST AGAINST THE

NOMINATION OF GEN. SCOTT,

FOR THE PRESIDENCY,

AND TO RECOMMEND

HON. DANIEL WEBSTER

FOR THAT OFFICE.

BOSTON:
PRINTED BY PRENTISS & SAWYER,
No. 11 Devonshire Street.
1852.

PROCEEDINGS.

AGREEABLY to a call very generally published in the journals of the city, a meeting of the citizens of the County of Suffolk, was held in Faneuil Hall, on Wednesday Evening, July 7, 1852, for the purpose of taking such measures as might be deemed proper, against sustaining the nominations made at the Baltimore Convention of Whigs, on the twenty-first of June. The meeting was enthusiastically responded to, there being present between four and five thousand persons.

Shortly after eight o'clock, the meeting was called to order by Mr. JOHN HAMMOND, and HENRY WILLIAMS, Esq., was chosen to preside over the meeting, and S. M. HOBBS, WM. B. MAY, and JAMES H. BLAKE, Esqs., were chosen Secretaries.

On taking the Chair, Mr. WILLIAMS briefly addressed the audience upon the object for which they had assembled. He reviewed the action of the Baltimore Convention, and showed conclusively, that until the last day's balloting there was a fair majority of the Convention opposed to the nomination of Gen. SCOTT, and that it was ultimately accomplished by the adroit management of aspiring politicians, who shamelessly set at naught the known wishes of a vast majority of the Whigs of the country. He counselled the Whigs to take courage, and go on in the good work of putting DANIEL WEBSTER in nomination as the candidate of the people for the Presidency.

Mr. WILLIAMS closed by comparing the frank, open position of Mr. WEBSTER, on the Compromise, with the "mum" policy of Gen. SCOTT, and criticised severely the course of Gen. SCOTT in relation to his letter to the Baltimore Convention.

His remarks were received with great applause.

Hubbard Winslow, Esq., was then introduced to the meeting, and spoke as follows : —

Mr. Chairman and Fellow Citizens :

No man can regret more sincerely than I do, the necessity which has called this meeting. I had hoped that before this time we should have been assembled to *ratify* the nomination of the man for whom the people wish to vote for our Chief Magistrate. But a previous and momentous duty is still before us. We have assembled as fellow citizens, bound together by ties far dearer and more sacred than those of party, not to shed vain tears over lost hopes, nor to eulogise one whom we tamely allow to be publicly dishonored We mean to do something to the purpose.

We have come, not to *bury* Cæsar, not to *praise* him, for he is not dead, and our praise he does not need. We have come together to do what we can, in connection with the great people of the land, to place a greater and more deserving than Cæsar in a position higher than Rome could offer. We have come to say, that the enlightened people of this Republic can appreciate true greatness, that they know how to be grateful, and will demonstrate both to the world. We have come to re-utter the Declaration of Independence, to say that the people of this land are free, and that they will, without regard to political parties, as true Americans, elevate to their highest office the greatest Statesman, the firmest and most tried pillar, and the brightest living ornament of the nation. In short, we have come to say that DANIEL WEBSTER ought to be, and we hope, will be, by the loud acclaim of a free and patriotic people, President of the United States.

Gentlemen, louder notes than ours will yet be struck in every part of the land. As the voice of many waters and of mighty thunderings, as the jubilant pæan of angels, they will roll from sea to sea, proclaiming Daniel Webster the nation's choice ; and all the people will say, Amen.

We bring no railing accusations against the Baltimore Convention. Many there did nobly ; and all praise to the valiant hearts of the old Bay State, who survived fifty assaults against fearful odds, and were only outnumbered, not conquered, at last. Temporary defeat is in such cases the signal for ultimate victory. Remember the events of Bunker Hill. Shoulder to shoulder with each other, and breast to breast with their antagonists did the invincible heroes struggle on, until their ammunition, not their hearts, failing; their numbers, not their strength, surpassed; they prudently retired from the conflict.

But it was a dear-bought victory for the enemy. It roused up and concentrated the energies of the indignant people of the land to assert their rights and to challenge and establish their independence. So it will prove now. Those who have begun to flatter themselves, and to burn gunpowder, with the expectation that the intelligent people of this country will abide the decision of the Baltimore Convention, have not duly appreciated the American intellect, nor studied the American character. Leviathan is not so tamed. The American people have had to take their salvation into their own hands before; and they know how to do it again. DANIEL, too, has been before in the lion's den; but he came forth unharmed by the hand of an unseen Deliverer. So he will do again.

It is enough to say that the real sentiments of the majority of the people were not represented in that Convention. A singular combination of untoward circumstances within, conspired with improper influences from without, to bring matters to a bad issue, to place Mr. WEBSTER in a false position before the world, and thus to perpetrate a great personal wrong upon him and disgrace upon the country.

The only appeal now, is to the people, and that appeal will be made. This is in strict accordance with the spirit of the Constitution; as no man can doubt who studies that instrument. It is indeed our only ultimate protection from the action of wire-pullers, office-seekers, demagogues, and venal magistrates. Mr. TOOMBS, of Georgia, said rightly, "All real control in the nomination of a chief magistrate has been taken out of the hands of the people and placed in those of unauthorised political juntos. The Constitution in this respect has been subverted."

We now propose, gentlemen, to fall back upon the Constitution and to abide strictly by it; to eschew all party; and to appeal boldly to the free and independent citizens of the Republic. This appeal is without the knowledge of Mr. WEBSTER. He may not like it. That cannot be helped. He has so long and earnestly taught us to obey the Constitution that he ought not to complain if we have learned the lesson and are ready to recite it. He has become the property of the nation, and must submit to its disposal. Perhaps he deserves some rebuke for his seeming indifference to our anxieties. That he could be slumbering so soundly through the night, to be prepared, as usual, to "learn the morning hour from the constellations, and to spring upward with the lark to greet the purpling east with blithe and jocund spirit," while we were in a wakeful agony of suspense, is almost provoking. And yet how such a spirit enhances the beauty of true greatness.

But we shall not soon forget the thronging multitudes of State Street, awaiting with almost breathless solicitude the repeated throbbings of those impassioned wires; nor the deep gloom that settled on all faces, and seemed to pervade the entire city and country around us, when the final announcement came. The shock of an earthquake would not have been more appalling. Never did the lightnings play so terribly on those mysterious rods.

Mr. Chairman, we come to offer no rude complaints against the gentleman whom the Convention have nominated for the Presidency; much less to countenance those despicable arts of detraction, by which low and vulgar minds of one party seek to heap ridicule upon the candidate of another. Shame on such infamous measures! They who must needs join issue between a "hasty plate of soup," on the one hand, and a "Pierce-ing cry," on the other, must be reduced to wretched poverty of argument, or be in a pitiable state of mental imbecility.

Franklin Pierce, I have no doubt, is a most worthy and excellent citizen. From all that I have learned of him, he is a truly amiable and upright man, and one whom, were there no person having a higher claim to the Presidency, I should not hesitate to support. But I cannot doubt that he himself really knows that the Presidency belongs, at least for the next four years, to his elder and more experienced brother of the Granite State. I hope he will yet see his way clear to vote for him. If he should, I will, for once in my life, make a bargain, and agree to vote for him next time.

And as for Winfield Scott, who ought not to be loud in his praise? He is, unquestionably, one of the most accomplished Generals of the nation. He has rendered service to his country that should honor him in all American hearts. He ought not to be President, for this one reason, if no more, that he is wanted in another sphere, — a sphere for which he has been trained from childhood, and in which he eminently shines. What would you think of placing Daniel Webster at the head of an important military campaign or battle, when Gen. Scott was at your service? And for a similar reason, what ought you to think of placing General Scott to preside over and decide upon the deliberative councils of State, when Daniel Webster is at your service? Why should common sense desert us in a case so plain? Let each have his own place — let each contribute to the salvation and glory of the land, by filling the station for which nature and education and long experience, have signally prepared him. If illustrious valor is wanted on the field, not less so is profound statemanship in the national councils. *Parvi sunt foris arma, nisi est consilium domi.*

But there are other invincible reasons why WINFIELD SCOTT ought not to take the direction of the nation's councils, and why wise and considerate men should be slow to sustain him. Those great questions which have long and fearfully agitated the nation to its centre, and even threatened the very dissolution of the Union, were at length, by the highest and most intense devotion to the nation's intellect, constitutionally adjusted in the measures of the well known Compromise Bill. Of this bill, DANIEL WEBSTER, with the concurrence of HENRY CLAY and other profound statesmen, was the author. Standing firmly on the pillars of the Constitution, amidst the tumultuous conflict of popular sentiment, he settled principles of duty and plans of action to perpetuate the Union, harmonise contending interests, and safely conduct the nation to future greatness and repose.

Of the important principles and plans here divulged, every intelligent citizen in the land soon had a well defined and settled opinion — and every man, not timidly sensitive to the popular breath, or a slave to public sentiments, boldly avowed and maintained it. And yet, up to the very hour when they were about to canvass at Baltimore, General SCOTT, who has never been suspected of wanting courage on the battle-field, had ventured no opinion and taken no ground on these momentous subjects; — and even then, it only appeared, that there was a private letter, in a certain friend's breeches pocket, in which he had expressed a willingness, if his friends judged it expedient, to endorse the sentiments of the Compromise, in case the Convention wished it as the condition of his nomination! What say you to that, gentlemen? What will the South and the West, so deeply interested in the bill, say to it? We know what they will say — what they have begun to say already. Is *this* the man to be entrusted with the nation's councils? Will you put *him* at the head of the nation, who has already put himself into his friend's breeches pocket?

I do not detract an iota from his appropriate honor. My complaint of him is, that he does not for a moment make a truce with his vanity just enough to see that the Presidential Chair is not the place for him. He is a coward in State councils, only because he is here out of his place. And, indeed, anything but cowardice must be what is still worse, fool-daring. For when a man is in a place in which he does not know how to act, unless he has the sense to get out of it, what remains for him but to be the tool of others, or recklessly venturesome? Gen. SCOTT's conduct in the matter of the Compromise, only illustrates what all the world knows, that man is truly wise and is to be trusted only in his own calling. I do not know but Gen. SCOTT is as capable of conducting the helm of State through troublesome times, as DANIEL WEBSTER is of conducting a steamboat through stormy seas. But I would not trust either of them thus out of his place. Give us the experienced navigator to guide our ships, Gen. SCOTT to guide our armies, DANIEL WEBSTER to guide our State councils.

But we are told that Mr. WEBSTER is undoubtedly the best of all living men for a President, but is "*not available.*" I move, Sir, that those wicked words be put in chains for the remainder of the year '52. They have done mischief enough for one year. Let us appeal to the people, and see whether he is available. The people are not yet all fools, though wise politicians have tried hard to make them so. Give them a chance to speak for themselves on a comprehensive national ticket, and they will gloriously tell us what they know.

But, Sir, if the question turns on availability, Gen. SCOTT is a most unfortunate candidate. *The people will not choose him.* The Democracy are the majority of the people, and the scathing letters of Gen. JACKSON, whose word with them is law and gospel, are already on the wing. A distinguished gentleman of the Democratic party told me they would be circulated by millions, would penetrate all the mines of Pennsylvania, every cabin of the West and South, and would effectually annihilate him in the estimation of every Democrat in America. The same gentleman said, that while not a Democrat will vote for SCOTT, thousands of them are ready to vote for WEBSTER.

As to the Whigs, we are certain that a large proportion of them will not sustain SCOTT, whether WEBSTER is before them or not. His chance is therefore desperate. He is a Win-*field*, but will never be a win *vote*. Our only hope is in the nation's favorite, DANIEL WEBSTER, on a free Union ticket. To this let all true patriots turn their hearts.

Gentlemen, the humble individual who has the honor to address you, is an old-fashioned, WASHINGTON, HAMILTON, WEBSTER Whig. My earliest recollections are of HAMILTON, as represented in a wax figure, dying by the hands of AARON BURR. I was led to examine his writings and compare his views, subsequently, with those of WASHington, and more recently with those of Webster. Never did three men think more alike touching the true policy and interests of this Federal Republic. They are the bright trio, the Orion belt of our firmament — let the principles which they inculcated be firmly sustained, and our Republic will last as long and shine as brilliantly as the glorious constellation which these advocates represent.

Nor do we forget John C. Calhoun. A nobler spirit never honored our nation's councils. If he sometimes favors a little too much his own State, and not enough the entire Union, it was the venial fault of an affectionate father, who loved his own children best. The error, if one it was, was lost in the flooding glories of his whole public and private life. He truly loved the nation and died for its interests — what few men have been able to do. Our hearts would have rejoiced to see him President of the United States.

Let it not be counted a sacrilege so soon to touch the ashes of Henry Clay. Immortal life is breathed into them, and they belong to the nation. His ascended spirit looks from its imperial throne over the land which his illustrious life and labors blessed, and his sympathies are all with us. He was nominated for the Presidency, but was defeated by corruption at the polls. A wound was inflicted upon our hearts which can never be healed but by the elevation of his twin brother in glory. Let the united honors be theirs; if, indeed, honor can be conferred on men who, like the sun, seem only capable of shedding lustre on the land without receiving any addition to their own. Let Henry Clay be enshrined in our hearts as the man whom we desired for our President, and let him be perpetuated and embodied in all that is mortal and immortal of Daniel Webster as the man we secured. O what a balm of consolation for a nation of weeping hearts!

And, gentlemen, must those three greatest of the men of this generation descend to their graves, without giving the honor of one of their names to the Presidential office? Must the only survivor of the three be allowed to pass away without the people even being allowed a *chance* to vote for him? God forbid! No! Invoking the aid of Him who rules the destinies of nations, we say deliberately and firmly, *it shall not be!* Daniel Webster will be placed before the great and sovereign people of the nation, in his untrammeled greatness, in all the lustre of his living self, and every voter who knows his right hand from his left, shall have a chance to choose him. If the Whig party has not the sense nor the ability even to *nominate* him; if it thus ungratefully abandons its greatest and truest friend, to whom it owes infinitely more than to any other living man, there is folly and corruption in its ranks; it has ceased to be what it was; its glory has departed; salvation shall come from another source. AND COME IT WILL! Thanks to Heaven! we live in a free government, after all; and the people will rule.

Nor can we fail to speak, in terms of unqualified admiration, of the present incumbent of the Presidential chair. His consistent and dignified course, his fidelity to all the great interests reposed in him, have won him the nation's lasting gratitude. But as he has had his turn of service, no man feels more deeply than himself that the place now belongs to his illustrious senior in years and service. He was ready at any moment, during the session of the Convention, to give him the preference.

Vinsi quam vincere maluit.

This noble spirit has won him imperishable laurels in all parts of the land.

And now, Mr. Chairman and gentlemen, as other speakers are to succeed me, I ought to release your attention. Allow me, before closing, briefly to state a few of the many reasons why measures should be immediately taken to bring Mr. WEBSTER before the people.

1. The decision of the Baltimore Convention *was not a true exponent of the wishes of the great body of the people.* We have abundant facts to prove this, but time forbids me here to divulge them. They will be forthcoming when needed. As the people were not represented there, it is constitutional and right to take measures by which they may represent themselves in another way.

2. The Presidency of the United States, all admit, *clearly belongs to Mr. Webster.* He has abundantly *earned* it, by a long life of intense self-sacrificing and successful public service. The service of no other living man can compare with his. He has saved us from wars abroad, and distractions at home; he has stretched his broad arms from Maine to Georgia, and from the Atlantic to the Pacific, and held us together as a nation; his wisdom has permeated and expounded, and his eloquence has defended the Constitution of the Union; the grandeur of his intellect and the power of his State-logic, has given us character and importance in foreign lands; and he has done all with unparalleled steadfastness and singleness of aim to the permanent welfare and glory of the entire nation.

A fraction of his time, with his commanding powers at the bar, might have lavished wealth upon him. He might have lived in comparative ease and luxury; he might have reposed in gardens of pleasure, or revelled in the sweets of refined literature; he might have retired, with ample means, to pass the evening of his days on his beloved farm, there, surrounded with all that earth can give, to sing with his favorite bard of Mantua —

> O fortunatos nimium, sua si bona novint,
> Agricolas ! quibus ipsa, procul discordibus armis,
> Gundit humo facilem victum, justissima tellus.

But no; he has laid his great talents, his whole life, all he has, and is upon the altar of his country's welfare. He is father and guardian of an entire generation, and shall he now in his advanced years, be set aside by the very children whom he has thus loved and blessed. Patriotic young men of Boston, what do you say? What you say will be responded by the young men of other cities all over the land.

3. Mr. WEBSTER *lives in the hearts of all true American Unionists.* All true friends of their country love and honor him with an affection transcending the bounds of party. Hence he will command a large vote from the noble-hearted Democrats. A gentleman of high standing and influence, who has held important offices of State, said to me yesterday, "I have always been a firm Democrat of the old school; if the choice lies between SCOTT and PIERCE, I shall, of course, vote for PIERCE, but if DANIEL WEBSTER is brought before the people, I shall vote for him. It is a disgrace," said he, "not only to the Whig party, but to our whole country, to have such a glorious man set aside."

And, Sir, this is the feeling of multitudes of that political creed. All parties are waking up to this subject; the national pride is touched; such enthusiasm will soon be developed all over the land as has not been realized since WASHINGTON took the chair.

A gentleman from New York City said to me yesterday, "New York will never submit to the nomination at Baltimore — *never! — never!* Begin in Boston — let the old Cradle of Liberty again rock the Genius of Independence, and we are ready to follow you. *Bring Daniel Webster forward, and we are with you.*"

Sir, the eyes of all are now turning to Massachusetts. They expect us to take the lead. It is not the first struggle by which Massachusetts has led the nation to victory and glory. That Bunker Hill Monument, whose foundation and whose cap-stone were laid amidst the thundering voices of the people, responded to patriotic eloquence of the American statesman, has yet another victory to commemorate.

4. Leaving Mr. Fillmore out of the account, Mr. Webster is the *only man who can command the votes of the South.* The South well knows what Mr. Webster has done and suffered for it, and its warm and generous heart knows how to be grateful. That heart has not been spoken. More than a hundred of the Southern delegates at the Convention were ready at any moment to vote for his nomination, but were kept back, temporarily, from motives of policy. They are now ready. Already, tidings have reached us, that their throbbing hearts are about to speak, and when the utterance comes, it will be as a prolonged and mighty peal of thunder, set to the tune of *Hail Columbia.* And a voice will be heard, as the voice of a trumpet, proclaiming, "Say to the North, give up, and to the South, keep not back. Maine and Georgia will hear it and obey." A voice from the Toombs of Georgia has already reached us.

5. The succession of Mr. Webster to Mr. Fillmore will occasion no jar in the present administration. There will be no turning of men out of office, to make room for political friends. He will enter upon his office unpledged to a single being; and all who know him (and who does not?) knows that even his opponents have nothing to fear from him. A truly magnanimous mind, like his, is incapable of revenge. He knows only how to overcome evil with good. This fact will be of great service in securing the coöperation of those who might otherwise wish to defeat his election. Those who are now anxious to bring Mr. Webster before the people are not office-seekers; nor will they be office-holders. For my humble self, with my present position and feelings, nothing could induce me to accept any office in the power of Government to bestow. And I know this to be true of the great body of gentlemen who wish to wipe away a disgrace from the nation. Let those in office who opposed Mr. Webster's nomination from this time only allow *justice* to be done, and not a hair of their heads will perish.

Mr. Webster's great work as President of the United States would be, we all know from his past course, to carry out faithfully the present administration, in which he is engaged; to fulfil all the conditions of the Compromise; to establish and confirm the Union on the broad basis of the Constitution; to settle, definitely and forever, the delicate points of our foreign as well as domestic relations; to protect our industry and our commerce; to take the direction of matters from the hands of selfish politicians, and establish constitutional rights; to institute a judicious and equitable tariff, that will at once defend us from dangerous monopolies, and protect the rights of the middling classes and of the laboring classes; to foster institutions of learning, and to encourage internal improvements; in a word, to lead the nation steadily onward to that elevation and security and glory, which shall realize the immortal WASHINGTON'S dying vision of the future Republic of America.

6. As Mr. WEBSTER belongs to the nation, the people of the land owe it to themselves, not less than to him, *to take him triumphantly out of the hands of his revilers.* So they did in the case of WASHINGTON; for he too had his enemies and traducers. By placing him where they did, they at length silenced the tongue of slander, set him in the clear upper sky, and handed him down to posterity with a name that an angel might envy. The same duty devolves on us, in relation to our present WASHINGTON.

I cannot claim the honor of an intimate personal acquaintance with Mr. WEBSTER. Were I disposed to envy any body, I should certainly envy those who have that honor. My only knowledge of him is from his doings and writings, which are before the world.

But, Sir, I have the honor of a personal acquaintance with gentlemen of the highest and most delicate integrity who *do* know him most intimately, and who have been with him early and late, and at all times — in seasons most free and unconstrained, and in hours of temptation most trying — who solemnly declare that a man of purer mind and more correct habits they never knew.

"No other living man," if I may use the language of your excellent Mayor in a personal conversation — "has been so shamefully slandered." Not only his public acts, but even his private character, has been assailed. Gentlemen, you understand me. Miserable, contemptible abuse! Spawn of envy and malice! *Male suoit qui male pense.* Or, to put a more charitable construction, the pitiable artifice of little and vain minds, that think to add something to themselves by plucking a wreath from a great man's brow. Every man of common sense ought to *know* better than to believe this slander.

The man who can do what Mr. WEBSTER has done, through every day of a long and most laborious life; who can rise with the lark, sustain from ten to fifteen hours a day of most responsible and exhausting mental effort, and yet be ever ready to welcome his friends with the same cheerful serenity; who could elicit and put forth those volumes of profound and masterly thought, chaste and classical diction, elevated and splendid imagery, which have done more than any other writings to stamp an intellectual character upon America; who could conduct the most involved and difficult negotiations that ever engaged the human mind, with a calmness, clearness, steadiness, and comprehensiveness that never failed of success; who has actually borne, for a quarter of a century, the whole nation, President and all, upon his shoulders — I say, the man who can do all this, without both intellectual and physical habits of the highest order, *must be more than human.* All this DANIEL WEBSTER HAS DONE; and it is high time that the intelligent citizens of this land have an opportunity to tell the world and posterity how they regard him.

But it is said, "Mr. WEBSTER is *admired* by all, but is not *popular.*" So said to me this day a gentleman whom I greatly honor. *Not popular?* with *whom?* with political demagogues; — with certain designing spirits that hover about conventions; with office-seekers; with men of low ambition at Washington; who wish for President a man whom they can *use* — a tool — one that knows even less of State councils than themselves — a President whose chief glory and defence must be in doing just as they bid him. They well know that DANIEL WEBSTER is not that man; therefore he is with them unpopular. For this very reason we wish to take him out of their hands and place him where he belongs, — in the hands of the people.

7. My final reason for action is, that this *is our last chance.* If Mr. WEBSTER is not our next President, he *never will be* our President. The die is cast forever! And, Sir, although he can afford to do without us, we cannot afford to do without him. He may, with only a *weeping* heart, leave us, but we with nothing less than *bleeding* hearts can leave him. If he now retires from the councils of the nation of which he has so long been the leading mind, it will be to cast a lingering eye of sadness upon our folly, and to grieve at our errors and our misrule, and I fear to find too early a grave. But give him this object to live for, let his long and brilliant career culminate in the proclaimed voice of the nation making him its chief magistrate, and the most useful and illustrious years of his life yet await him; for man is immortal, so long as their remains a work for him.

On retiring from the Presidency, after four years of service, he will let fall his mantle upon a worthy successor, and the people, blessed with his example and his counsels, will forever know what kind of a man it is best to choose to preside over the nation. They will have learned a lesson never to be forgotten — a lesson that will protect the dignity of office and the honor of the nation. And when, many years hence, every avenue that leads to the tomb of Marshfield shall be trodden hard, strangers from distant lands will not need to be told that it was done by the feet of grateful and admiring people going to pay the homage of their tears over the dust of their second WASHINGTON.

Mr. Chairman and gentlemen, I conclude as I began, with saying, as the sense of this meeting, that DANIEL WEBSTER OUGHT TO BE, AND, GOD HELPING, WILL BE, THE NEXT PRESIDENT OF THE UNITED STATES.

[During the delivery of the above most eloquent and powerful address, Mr. WINSLOW was repeatedly honored with the most earnest and enthusiastic applause. The address was listened to with profound and gratifying attention.]

The following Preamble and Resolutions were then read, at the request of the Chairman, by Mr. WINSLOW.

WHEREAS, We believe that though the policy of holding Conventions for the purpose of uniting political parties and concentrating their action, is, in principle, a sound one, and that the doings of such Conventions, when in accordance with the clearly expressed wishes and sentiments of their constituents, are obligatory upon them, yet, we further believe, that unless such regard is paid in the selection of candidates for office, to the well-known preferences of those represented, the action of Conventions is *morally* and *politically* of no binding force;

AND, WHEREAS, We believe that, in the recent nomination of Gen. SCOTT, at the Baltimore Convention, the undoubted sentiments of a large majority of the Whig Party throughout the Union have been utterly disregarded, and that the Convention, in calling upon Whigs to give their support to this nomination, are asking them to vote for one who is, undeniably, NOT the man of their choice; — moreover, that in so doing, they further ask them to set aside a candidate of vastly superior abilities and qualifications for the office;

AND WHEREAS, The present occasion is one more favorable than will be likely again to occur, for entering a general protest against a nomination made so directly in opposition to the *common sense*, *patriotism*, and *intelligence* of the Whig Party, and of the whole American People, therefore,

RESOLVED, That the Whigs of Massachusetts have received the announcement of General SCOTT'S nomination with *deep chagrin* and *disappointment*, and that, as a party, we feel absolved from all obligation to support his nomination; that no considerations of *expediency*, or of the *imagined* interests of the party, shall make us swerve from our fixed determination to oppose his election by every lawful means in our power; and that, in pursuance of this purpose, we will unite with all good men of our party, and of the other parties of our country, in taking measures to place in nomination the greatest of America's sons next to the immortal Washington — a candidate who, from his surpassing talents, his long-tried public services, his patriotic feelings, and his unequalled statesmanship, is commended to the nation as more worthy of the high office of the Chief Magistracy of the United States, and better fitted to perform its duties, than ANY OTHER MAN.

RESOLVED, That in the recent decease of the Hon. HENRY CLAY, the nation has lost a *profound statesman, an unswerving patriot, and a great man;* and that, while this event fills us with profound emotions of grief, we are, at the same time, admonished that of that glorious triumvirate of statesmen, which has controlled and directed, more than all others, for the last forty years, the political destinies of our country, there now remains but ONE — *the greatest of all* — and that an opportunity is now offered — and the *last* — when a grateful people may show that they can as well appreciate and reward *civil* greatness and intellectual superiority, as that commoner quality, military valor.

RESOLVED, That the great mass of the people are ever true in their instincts, and ever to be trusted, and that those who fear to commit their cause to the decision of this tribunal, and who seek to dictate to them whom they shall choose as President of the United States, in utter disregard of their known feelings and judgment as to who would, most *worthily* in himself and most *honorably* to the nation occupy that place, should be, for once, made to feel, by an earnest protest at the ballot-box, which shall be heard from MAINE to CALIFORNIA, that, despite the fears and intrigues of party politicians, *the people* can be depended upon to make their own selections of suitable candidates, and to vindicate the nation from the charge that "REPUBLICS ARE EVER UNGRATEFUL."

Resolved, That, in denying the "*availability*" of the most eminent statesman of the day, the *proudest intellect of the age*, DANIEL WEBSTER, they who doubt the success which such a candidate would meet with from the hands of the American People, show a want of confidence in their ability to appreciate greatness like his, as well as in their gratitude for his services and enthusiastic admiration for the man, which they, by their eager zeal to promote his election, should an opportunity be afforded them, *will indignantly rebuke.*

Resolved, That we have full faith, not only in the "*availability*" of DANIEL WEBSTER, but in the triumphant success which awaits the party that shall put his name before the people, as a Candidate for the office of President; and that we hasten to spread out to the breeze the standard inscribed with his name; confident that it will be greeted with acclamations throughout the country; and that, under its folds, we shall be led on to a TRIUMPHANT AND SUCCESSFUL RESULT.

Resolved, finally, That to promote the objects specified in the foregoing Preamble and Resolutions, measures be at once taken by this meeting for causing a Convention of those favorable to the nomination of the Hon. DANIEL WEBSTER, without distinction of party, to be called at an early day, and that ——— be a Committee to prepare and circulate a suitable Address to the friends of Mr. WEBSTER, in all the States of the Union, inviting and urging their hearty and strenuous coöperation with us for the accomplishment of the noble and glorious purpose we have in view.

Horace H. Day, Esq., was then called upon to say a few words. He said in substance: —

Mr. Chairman and Gentlemen, — The same intelligence which induces me to prefer the greatest man of the age as the candidate for the Presidency, will induce me to abstain from attempting here, and now, a speech, at this late hour. I do not wish to mar the beautiful, patriotic, and intelligent address, to which we have all listened with so much pleasure, from your chosen speaker. I heartily endorse the sentiments of that address. I did not come here prepared to make a speech. It is gratifying to witness the absence of mere politicians from this meeting, and the spontaneous rising of the *people*, who are in no wise influenced by wire-pulling. I rejoice to have this night seen Faneuil Hall filled, crowded, every nook and corner, even every window-niche and standing-place, crammed with such an enlightened, intelligent, orderly, and enthusiastic body of Massachusetts Whigs and freemen. I know and feel what brought you here to-night.

I intend to say but one word. I live in the patriotic State of New Jersey. The nomination of Gen. Scott does not meet the approval of the body of Jersey Whigs. Indeed, the State of New Jersey was misrepresented in the Baltimore Convention, and, mark my word, the ides of November will so prove.

The above Resolutions were now unanimously passed.

It was then *Voted*, that when the meeting adjourn, it adjourn to meet again on Wednesday Evening, July 14, at eight o'clock, to consider an Address to the people of the United States, and take measures to secure the election of Mr. Webster.

Messrs. William Hayden, Tolman Willey, Hubbard Winslow, Henry Williams, George Darracott, and James H. Blake, were chosen a Committee of Correspondence, and to prepare a suitable Address to the people, of all parties, of the United States.

The meeting then adjourned to assemble at the same place on the evening of the fourteenth of July.

HENRY WILLIAMS, *Chairman.*

S. M. Hobbs,
William B. May, } *Secretaries.*
James H. Blake,

ADJOURNED MEETING.

In accordance with the vote passed on the seventh instant, the Whigs of the County of Suffolk, opposed to the nomination of the Baltimore Convention, met in Faneuil Hall, on the evening of Wednesday, the fourteenth of July. At half past eight o'clock, Henry Williams, Esq., took the Chair. The Hall was nearly full. He proceeded to address the meeting, in furtherance of the object for which it had met, and alluded to the measures which had been taken by the leaders in this movement to ensure the nomination of Mr. Webster. He remarked that the measure first originated in Boston. He also objected to the movement made to call a convention at Philadelphia, in August. It should have been deferred until things were ready for such a movement. After this meeting, active measures were to be taken to ensure a convention which would command respect. Mr. Williams administered a stern and deserved rebuke to the faint-hearted supporters of Mr. Webster. He closed by urging firmness on the part of those engaged in the cause, and believed it would yet result gloriously, and announcing that an "Address to the people of the United States" had been prepared, and would be submitted during the evening.

There was now a general call for Hubbard Winslow, Esq., in response to which that gentleman spoke at great length and with masterly ability. He was particularly happy in descanting upon, and defining the true powers of nominating Conventions. He was fully of opinion, and demonstrated to the entire satisfaction of his auditory, that such was the action and the means resorted to, to procure the nomination of Gen. Scott by the Baltimore Convention, that no true Whig was, in honor or good faith, bound to support that gentleman. He made a very strong argument against the policy of a resort to mere military men, to the exclusion of accomplished and experienced civilians, who had spent their lives in devotion to the affairs of State, and whose patriotism was, beyond all doubt, fully established. Mr. WINSLOW closed by an earnest and thrilling appeal to devoted friends of the country, of all political parties, "to put their shoulders to the wheels," even at this late day, to unite their energies for the great and righteous object of putting in nomination the man of the people's choice, the Hon. DANIEL WEBSTER. More than this, he expressed a strong conviction that the case was not so desperate as to preclude a chance of ultimate success.

By request of the Chairman, Mr. WINSLOW then read the following

ADDRESS

TO THE PEOPLE OF THE UNITED STATES.

A numerous gathering of the citizens of Boston, who are dissatisfied with the nomination made by the Whig party at the recent Convention held in Baltimore, hereby present the name of

DANIEL WEBSTER,

as a candidate, independent of party, for the office of President of the United States.

We take this step in no factious spirit; we are not impelled to it by any motives of self-interest; we are neither politicians, nor seekers after office; we have no ends to serve which separate us, in any manner, from our fellow citizens; but we have looked upon the action of the Whig Convention with deep sorrow, — with bitter regret, — and we feel called upon, by a sense of duty higher than allegiance to party, to enter our protest against that action, and publicly to avow our determination, not only *not* to sustain it, but to do whatever lies in our power to elect the man who should have been its candidate, and who *would* have been its candidate had not the good sense of the great mass of the Whig party been circumvented by a few *designing, cold-blooded, selfish politicians!*

Fellow Citizens: — Under ordinary circumstances — against the candidates of the two great political parties — an independent nomination, we are well aware, would be of no avail. But we say, and the people of the United States, of all parties, will bear witness to the truth of our assertion, that neither of the names offered for your suffrages are such as should have been presented at this time. We ask you to consider whether the election of either the Whig or Democratic candidate will tend to promote the best interest of our common country, to give it a commanding position before the world, or encourage the friends of freedom in other lands to struggle for the triumph of the "divine right" of self-government? Whether, in fact, the election of either of the party candidates will not tend to weaken our own confidence in our own institutions, and to strengthen the hands of tyranny in the old world.

We make this nomination then, under no ordinary circumstances, nor for any ordinary purpose. We present the name of a man for your suffrages who commands the respect, the esteem, and the admiration of every patriotic citizen of our broad land, be his party predilections what they may; who commands the entire confidence of men of all parties at home, and who stands before the world as the greatest statesman of the age. We believe that the discontent with the nominations of both the great parties is wide-spread, deep, and well-founded; and that if every man who agrees with us in opinion will for once throw aside the trammels of party, and vote according to the dictate of his own unbiased judgment, success may attend us. We call, therefore, upon all such men to unite with us upon this great issue. We appeal to their patriotism, their love of country, and of the Union; their regard for liberty and the right of self-government; their national pride and their own best interest, to join in one well-concerted effort to place DANIEL WEBSTER in the Presidential Chair.

And why should not this effort be made? Why should the intelligent people of this great country bend in slavish submission to the behests of a few men who make politics a trade, and use the political machinery of party organizations merely to serve their own interest; whose artful management has thrust aside the greatest men of both parties, and who have now for the fourth time declared, that neither talents, nor statemanship, nor patriotism, nor integrity, nor a long life ardently devoted to the public service shall be taken into consideration in the selection of our Chief Magistrate?

Why should not this effort be made, when we know that it is eminently right? That in making it we are performing a high and a holy duty, and that whether it be crowned by success or not every man who lends it his aid will have the heartfelt satisfaction of knowing that victory will be a glorious triumph indeed, but that no dishonor will follow defeat.

In this effort we earnestly ask the coöperation of our fellow-citizens in other States who think as we do; of all those who prefer country to party, and who have moral courage enough to express that preference. We are ready to meet with them at any time and at any place, to consult and combine with them; to do whatever may be done to redeem the errors of party leaders, and to place our country in the proud position she ought to occupy before the world.

TO OUR FELLOW CITIZENS OF MASSACHUSETTS

We say, that it is owing, in some measure, to the influence exerted at Baltimore, by the false hearts and the false tongues of some of our own politicians, that DANIEL WEBSTER is not now the candidate of the Whig party. For were not those hearts false which expressed their own preference for him while they insidiously used every effort against him? And were not those tongues false which declared that DANIEL WEBSTER could not carry the electoral votes of his own State?

It is owing in part, also, to the action of two of our own delegates in that Convention, that our great statesman was thrust aside to make way for a mere military chieftain:—to the vote of one of them who expressed a strong preference for Mr. WEBSTER, and yet voted against him fifty-three times, on the poor pretence that he is not popular with the people! And to the vote of another who "could not *conscientiously* support the *man* who made that seventh of March speech," even after he had openly declared, as he had in that Convention, that the doctrines of that speech are all right and true, and that they stand—and must stand—as the corner-stone of our Union. It is because we have been thus misrepresented, and because our State has been thus slandered by some of our own fellow citizens, that we feel called upon to speak out as we have spoken, without waiting the action of other States.

There are thousands amongst us — Whigs and Democrats — who will not give their votes to either of the party candidates; thousands of all parties who earnestly desire to express their disapproval of the political trickery which has set aside the greatest name in our country — the greatest living man in the world: — thousands, who, if they do no more, will refrain from casting their votes at the coming election. To all such we say, that silence is not enough; to abstain from voting is the next thing to supporting candidates to whose election we are opposed; let us, therefore, express our disapprobation in such manner as to make it *tell*, and thus administer a rebuke to selfish schemers that will be remembered, and that will exercise a salutary influence hereafter. Let us go to the polls, one and all, and deposit our ballots for DANIEL WEBSTER.

Fellow Citizens! We shall be assailed by those who have brought us to this strait, if we thus dare to exercise our rights: we shall be denounced as traitors to the parties with which we have heretofore acted. Be it so; we can retort upon our assailants that they have been false to the trust reposed in them, — false to their party, — false to the Union, — false to the country, — false to the great interests of liberty and self-government throughout the world: and if evil comes of their action, let that evil rest upon their own heads. For ourselves, let us have no part nor lot in the matter, but in the independent exercise of our suffrage let us show to the world that we cannot be bought and sold, like sheep in the shambles, by a few unprincipled men whose desire to serve their own petty interests is their only rule of political action. Let us do our duty — our whole duty — like men who have principles of our own, and judgment of our own. Let us do what we can to remedy the wrongs inflicted upon our country by scheming politicians, and success *may* crown our efforts. Man *proposes*, but God *disposes:* let us act well our part and leave the event in humble trust to Him whose unsleeping eye is ever watching over us.

The above patriotic and able Address was accepted amid the earnest cheers of the large, enthusiastic, and respectable audience.

After further remarks from several gentlemen, the meeting was dissolved, with NINE CHEERS FOR DANIEL WEBSTER AND THE PRESIDENCY.

Throughout both meetings, though there were those present who evidently came for factious purposes, and were bent on making disturbance, there was manifested the strongest devotion and attachment to our distinguished candidate, Mr. Webster, and a fixed and unalterable determination to support him, at all hazards, and in no way or shape to countenance the nomination of Gen. Scott, whose position has been shown by his acts, and by his intriguing partizan and aspiring friends, as not the man who deserves the support of the American people for the highest office in their gift.

For the Committee,

HENRY WILLIAMS, *Chairman.*

S. M. Hobbs,
William B. May,
James H. Blake, } *Secretaries.*

Boston, July 14, 1852.

www.ingramcontent.com/pod-product-compliance
Lightning Source LLC
LaVergne TN
LVHW011142110826
845150LV00008B/2465
* 9 7 8 1 4 1 8 1 9 2 5 4 9 *